MONET

THE GREAT ARTISTS COLLECTION

MASON CREST

Contents

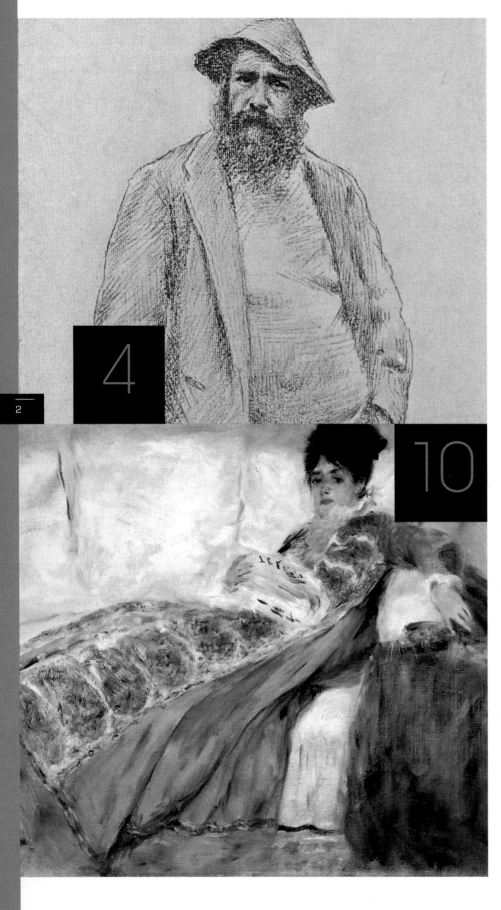

6 August to
26 October 2003

The Royal Bank
of Scotland

*Great Works order is alphabetical where possible.

Mason Crest
450 Parkway Drive, Suite D
Broomall, PA 19008
www.masoncrest.com

©2016 by Mason Crest, an imprint of National Highlights, Inc.

Printed and bound in the United States of America.

10 9 8 7 6 5 4 3 2

Cataloging-in-Publication Data on file with the Library of Congress.

Series ISBN: 978-1-4222-3256-9
Hardback ISBN: 978-1-4222-3261-3
ebook ISBN: 978-1-4222-8538-1

Written by: Tasha Stamford

Images courtesy of PA Photos and Scala Archives

"Everyone discusses my art and pretends to understand, as if it were necessary to understand, when it is simply necessary to love."
Claude Monet

Introduction

TH. ROBINSON
1890

■ **ABOVE: A portrait of Claude Monet by T. H Robinson, c. 1890.**

Monet is familiar to millions of people the world over. His works are much loved and admired so it's almost inconceivable to imagine that at the time he produced his first works, Monet enraged critics and the public alike. His paintings were often misunderstood and rejected by the Salon in Paris for their formal exhibitions. Without the support of the Salon, however, it was extremely difficult to become a recognized artist.

At times, the light Monet achieved in his paintings was almost the subject itself. The light enhanced the works and gave Monet's paintings a photographic quality, despite the "impression" of the subject of the piece. It was these impressions – rather than the subjects or themes – that established Monet as a revolutionary artist. Nothing like this had been seen prior to the 1870s and, to an established art world, this revolution was simply shocking.

Monet was the founder of the Impressionist movement and worked across more than six decades, to the point of obsession, to produce one of the largest volumes of oeuvres the world had ever seen. There are more than 2,050 paintings listed in the five-volume *Catalogue Raisonné* (1974-1991), by Daniel Wildenstein. Monet destroyed many of his own works that he was unsatisfied with, while others have been undoubtedly lost over time and do not appear in the catalogue. It is probably safe to say the actual number is much higher. Monet was known to cut, burn, or kick his work when it failed to meet his expectations and he was prone to bouts of depression and self-doubt.

Monet had developed his love of drawing from a young age while a student in Le Havre, France. He was a good pupil, but much preferred the outdoors and often filled his schoolbooks with sketches of people and caricatures of his teachers. He became well known for his sketches and drew many of the town's residents and, in 1859, moved to Paris, following the painful death of his mother two years earlier, to pursue his art. He became a student at the Académie Suisse and met fellow artist Camille Pissarro. While in Paris, Monet experienced painters copying from old masters but found he preferred to sit and paint what he saw.

The Impressionists were keen to eliminate the color black from their palettes and encouraged this practice at every opportunity. It brought about a new color theory – emphasizing the presence of color within shadows – and they worked to the rule that there was no black in nature, and therefore, it should not be included in their paintings. Monet is widely regarded as the forerunner of French Impressionism. He met Pierre-Auguste Renoir, Frédéric Bazille, and Alfred Sisley while studying in Paris with Charles Gleyre. It was these artists that discussed the effects of light with broken color created with rapid brushstrokes – a fundamental mark of Impressionism. Alongside Édouard Manet, Edgar Degas, and Renoir, Monet was keen for a move away from realism and the traditional oil painting techniques of the 19th century. It was early in his career that Monet created a style that concentrated on the light in shadows. This study of natural light was the focus of his first "Impressionist" painting, *Impression, Sunrise* (1872), which came to represent the new art movement taking

■ **ABOVE: A portrait of Camille Pissarro, a contemporary of Monet.**
■ **OPPOSITE: Édouard Manet pictured c. 1894.**
■ **BELOW: French Impressionist, Pierre-Auguste Renoir in his studio.**

shape. Louis Leroy, a critic who viewed the painting, was unsympathetic to the developments taking place in art toward the end of the 19th century and called the work an "impression." It was meant to ridicule Monet's work (and the work of his peers in general), however, it led to the naming of one of the most exciting movements and phases in art history – Impressionism.

The formidable Paris Salon rejected the work, *Impression, Sunrise*, and the new movement decided to hold its own shows. The first Impressionist exhibition took place in 1874 – a radical move by Monet and his fellow artists desperate to escape the "tyranny" of the traditional shows. Monet consistently explored how to further his own development. He became an advocate of plein air (outdoor) painting – leading to some of the most exquisite landscape works that captured real events and how they related to light. His works are beautiful, interesting, gentle, and tranquil – in keeping with a bourgeois background – but they are also emotional pieces that evoke understanding while providing aesthetic qualities that are simply breathtaking.

Monet exhibited his paintings at most of the Impressionist exhibitions and traveled fairly extensively, although he barely left Europe. More than any other artist, he was keen to further the Impressionist vision. His works range from "busy," bustling pieces depicting Paris life, to peaceful figures, large landscapes, and his beloved garden, especially the water lilies and pond which he created at his home in Giverny. The garden, and in particular the lilies, became the critical subject of his works toward the end of his life. Through analyzing Monet's works, it is possible to see his increasing preoccupation with color and atmospheric light effects. Richness and variety of colors replaced and overshadowed more conventional drawing and modeling of forms. Monet's father had not wished for his son to become an artist, but Jacques-François Ochard gave him his first drawing lessons, while the artist Eugène Boudin would become his mentor and teach him to use oil paints and techniques.

The Impressionists chose individualized responses to the modern world rather than the more traditional allegory or narrative subjects. They often painted with little or no preparatory study. They relied on their ability to draw and a myriad of colors. The human subject was favored by the likes of Manet, Degas, and Renoir, the latter of whom eventually turned to domestic life for inspiration. Renoir focused on the female nude. Monet, Pissarro, and Sisley preferred the countryside and landscapes for their primary motif. Weather was a major factor for these artists. Monet was the most prolific painter of the Impressionist movement and constantly challenged himself to further develop his style right up to the end of his life. The result was an enduring legacy.

(Mary Evans Picture Library)

(Mary Evans Picture Library)

■ **ABOVE:** Monet in his garden at Giverny.

■ **RIGHT:** Eugène Boudin's painting, *The Laundresses of Etretat.* Boudin would become Monet's mentor.

Monet

A Biography

(Mary Evans Picture Library)

■ **ABOVE:** **A self-portrait of Claude Monet, c. 1886.**

Oscar Claude Monet, known to his parents as Oscar, was born in Paris, on November 14, 1840. He was the second son of Claude Adolphe Monet and Louise Justine Aubrée Monet. At the age of five, Monet moved with his family to Le Havre in Normandy. He was expected to follow his father into the family green grocers but he was more interested in following his mother into the arts. Louise was a singer. He showed a talent for drawing from a young age and was enrolled at the Le Havre school of arts where

he became renowned for his caricatures – drawn in charcoal. He showed an acute business sense for a young schoolboy and sold the drawings for 10 francs (more if he could get it) to the locals. It was around this time that he met his mentor, Boudin, who taught him about en plein air techniques. Monet was hooked. He also became influenced by Johan Barthold Jongkind. In late January 1857, Monet's mother died. He was just 16 years old. He left school and went to live with his widowed, childless

(Public Domain)

■ **ABOVE: A self-portrait of Charles Gleyre who Monet studied with in Paris.**

■ **OPPOSITE: Camille Doncieux, 1866, *The Woman in the Green Dress*. Camille became Monet's wife and the mother of his children, as well as a favorite muse.**

aunt, Marie-Jeanne Lecadre.

From here Monet visited Paris where he was more influenced by painting what he saw than copying the old master in the Louvre like his young contemporaries. He stayed in Paris for a number of years and, in June 1861, joined the First Regiment of African Light Cavalry in Algeria. He signed up for seven years but was bought out by his aunt when he contracted typhoid fever two years later. In return for buying him out of the army, Monet's aunt expected him to enroll and complete a course at art school. Some commentators believe that Jongkind had some influence on this agreement. Monet, however, was not interested in the conventional and traditional schools of art and took up his studies with Charles Gleyre in Paris. It was then that he met his like-minded peers. He had met Manet on his first visit to Paris, but now he became associated with Renoir, Bazille, and Sisley. Monet became infatuated with his favorite muse, Camille Doncieux – who

(Mary Evans Picture Library)

■ **ABOVE:** A painting of Camille by Renoir: *Madame Monet lying on a sofa.*

later became his wife and the mother of his two sons. It was his painting *Camille*, also known as *The Woman in the Green Dress (La femme a la Robe Verte)*, in 1866, that was to bring his first real public recognition. Camille went on to pose for many of Monet's works – some where she is clearly recognizable and attributed, and other paintings where it is suspected that the woman figure in the paintings is her. Camille was certainly the figures for *Women in the Garden*, c. 1866 (where Monet copied the fashionable dresses of the day from magazines because he could not afford to clothe Camille in the

actual costumes). She also posed for *On the Bank of the Seine, Bennecourt*, two years later. Camille and Monet celebrated the birth of their first son, Jean, in 1867.

The couple fled to London, England, in September 1870 to escape the Franco-Prussian War that broke out on July 19 that same year. (Monet and Camille married in a civil ceremony on June 28, 1870.) In London, Monet became familiar with the works of William Turner and John Constable. Their landscapes would inspire the young Frenchman in his own innovations with color. However, in 1871, his works were rejected by the Royal

(Mary Evans Picture Library)

■ **ABOVE: Monet and his family settled in Argenteuil, a small town on the bank of the Seine, for seven years.**

Academy exhibition. The family moved to Holland in May 1871 – where Monet was suspected by the authorities of revolutionary activities. He created 25 works while in Zaandam and visited Amsterdam. Monet returned to France in October or November and settled in Argenteuil, a small town on the bank of the Seine, in December that year. Here he stayed for the next seven years (although he returned to Holland for a short visit in 1874), painting on the riverbank or in his boat studio.

Alongside *Impression, Sunrise*, in the 1874 Impressionist exhibition was one of two paintings of *Boulevard des Capucines*, although there is some speculation as to which one was actually included. While the family lived in Argenteuil, Monet painted a number of works depicting modern life. Camille, however, contracted tuberculosis and became seriously ill in 1876. Their second son, Michel, was born on March 17, 1878 and the family moved to Vétheuil. Here they lived alongside the Hoschedé family. Ernest Hoschedé was a wealthy businessman and patron of the arts. It was his wife, Alice, who would help Monet raise his sons in Vétheuil. Camille's fading health and established tuberculosis ended her life at the age of 32

■ **ABOVE: A painting of Vétheuil where Monet lived and raised his sons.**

■ **OPPOSITE: Monet's house at Giverny.**

on September 5, 1879. When Ernest went bankrupt he left for Belgium in 1878. It is suggested that between this time and Camille's death, Monet and Alice developed their relationship.

The following months proved a difficult time for Monet. The family had been living in great poverty for some time when Camille died, and a grief-stricken Monet vowed it would not continue. He dedicated his time to his work – leading, perhaps, to the greatest of his paintings of the 19th century. He was eager to document the French

countryside and seascapes and he embarked on campaigns that led to a series of paintings. Alice took Monet's sons to Paris to live alongside her own six children. The oldest, Blanche, eventually married Jean Monet. They rejoined Monet back in the countryside then the extended family moved to Poissy – which the artist hated – before they discovered Giverny in Normandy.

Giverny was first rented by the family (from 1883), but as Monet's reputation began to take off and the sales of his paintings – alongside careful and shrewd

18

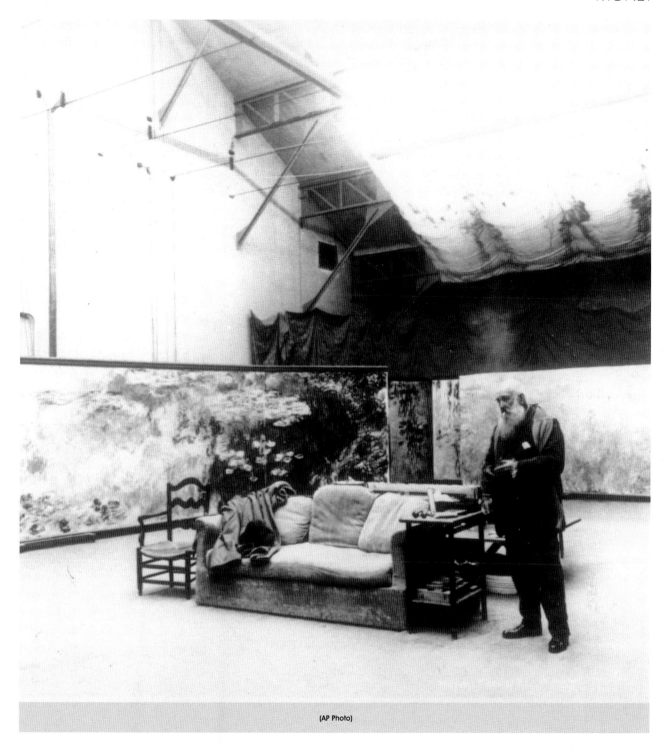

(AP Photo)

■ **ABOVE:** Monet in his studio at Giverny. Several of his works from the *Water Lilies* series can be seen along the walls.

■ **OPPOSITE:** Monet with writer Gustave Geffroy in his garden at Giverny, c. 1920.

investments – established his wealth, he was able to buy the house and gardens outright toward the end of the decade. (Following Ernest's death in 1892, Alice and Monet married.) The house came with land, a barn, which was used as a studio, orchards, and a small garden. The children were able to attend local schools and the surrounding countryside offered Monet his most favorite motif. During the 1890s, the gardens, which were already being built and developed, gained a greenhouse and a second studio. The first series that Monet created here was *Haystacks* (painted from different viewpoints at different times of the day). Other series followed, including *Rouen*

(PA Photos)

(Public Domain)

■ **ABOVE:** Giverny was left to the French Academy of Fine Art in 1966 and the house and gardens were opened to the public in 1980.

■ **OPPOSITE:** Monet on his estate at Giverny in a photograph dated 1923.

Cathedral, Poplar, Parliament, Mornings on the Seine and the *Water Lilies*.

Monet's garden flourished as his wealth grew. While he hired seven gardeners to look after the extensive grounds, he remained resolutely the garden's chief designer and architect. Monet's series of paintings from Venice are considered an extremely important contribution to his oeuvre. Alice died in 1911 and he lost his son, Jean, in 1914. It was Jean's wife, Blanche, who would come to

look after Monet when her mother died and the artist developed the first signs of cataracts. Weeping willows became his motif during the First World War (1914-1918) in which Michel Monet served, as did his father's friend Georges Clemenceau. The weeping willows were painted out of respect for France's fallen soldiers. Monet underwent operations on his eyes and some commentators argue that following these procedures he was able to see ultraviolet wavelengths of light that may have had an

(Mary Evans / Sueddeutsche Zeitung Photo)

effect on the colors he used – many of his water lilies were much bluer than they had been before. Nevertheless, he continued to work steadfastly until his death from lung cancer in 1926 at the age of 86. He was buried in the cemetery in Giverny in a small service as per his wishes.

Michel Monet left the house and gardens at Giverny to the French Academy of Fine Art in 1966. The Foundation Claude Monet opened the house and gardens to the public in 1980 after extensive restorations were carried out.

23

■ **LEFT:** Relaxing in his studio.
■ **BELOW:** *The Artist's Garden at Giverny*, 1902.

Great Works

Paintings

A Corner of the Apartment

(1875)

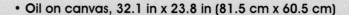

- **Oil on canvas, 32.1 in x 23.8 in (81.5 cm x 60.5 cm)**

Monet, Claude (1840-1926): Un coin d'appartement. Vue interieure avec le fils et la femme de l'artiste, 1875. Paris, Musee d'Orsay. peinture Dim. 0.8 x 0.6 m
© 2013. White Images/Scala, Florence

This exquisite work was completed when Monet was living with his family in the commune of Argenteuil in 1875. It is of Monet's oldest son, Jean, aged eight, and the artist's wife Camille sat ponderingly in the background. It was usual for Monet to paint his son and wife at this time and he has chosen a blue hue, which illuminates the child and continues across the parquet flooring. This helps to give the work perspective. The artist appears to be attempting the contrast between the darker interior and the light streaming through the window behind the small boy. It helps draw the audience's attention to the back of the piece and the window, table, and lamp. The child is framed by potted trees and plants in decorative blue and white Dutch urns, and colored motif drapes to the front of the painting that mirror the curtains surrounding the window. The figures give balance, one slightly in silhouette to the right, the other seated to the left. The colored motifs, green plants, and decorative pots were commonplace in Monet's work. The piece is tranquil and pays homage to everyday life. However, as Monet began to work with a passion en plein air, this type of subject would become increasingly rare.

A Field of Tulips in Holland

(1886)

• Oil on canvas, 25.6 in x 31.9 in (65 cm x 81 cm)

Monet, Claude (1840-1926): Champs de tulipes en Hollande, 1886. Paris, Musee d'Orsay. peinture Dim. 0.65 x 0.81 m. © 2013. White Images/Scala, Florence

Courting a Dutch windmill, this colorful scene was captured in tulip fields close to Sassenheim. It was the spring of 1886 and Monet created a classic Impressionist painting. From the brushstrokes, it would be hard to tell that the bursts of color are tulips, however, they clearly are these beautiful flowers, as is evident by the blocks of color, so typical of the way these flowers are grown. Monet was enchanted by these outdoor scenes – plein air – and has approached this everyday motif with gentleness and truth. The work was created on Monet's second visit to The Hague, although he stayed for just a short time in 1886. The tulip fields between Leiden and Haarlem inspired five works, though Monet found the scenes difficult to capture. *A Field of Tulips in Holland* clearly shows the changing light and color patterns that Monet sought to capture with the sunlight illuminating the blooms and the darker hues surrounding the buildings. This work was shown at the International exhibition in 1886 where the artist proved his success by selling all the paintings he submitted.

Argenteuil

(1872)

- Oil on canvas, 19.7 in x 25.6 in (50 cm x 65 cm)

Monet, Claude (1840-1926): Argenteuil, 1872. Paris, Musee d'Orsay. peinture Dim. 0.5 x 0.65 m. © 2013. White Images/Scala, Florence

Monet, Camille, and Jean escaped the Franco-Prussian war in 1870 by moving to London for a time. Here, the artist studied the works of Turner and Constable and the way in which they used light to conceal contours. Monet adopted the style in his own works, especially those that were completed during his time in Argenteuil where he set up a studio on a boat. This tranquil scene depicts Argenteuil to the left and the rolling hills of Orgemont in the background, over a subtle palette of calm waters. There are no bursts of color here; it is a peaceful and serene setting with gentle hues that almost give the impression of a light mist covering the work. The vegetation to the left, which extends through its reflection at the bottom of the work right through to the top of the trees, is also subtly created but balances perfectly with the land and hills that extend horizontally before rounding slightly forward to the right of the painting. The boats are particularly striking and their reflections add to their magnificence. However, when first unveiled to the public, there was little understanding for early Impressionism in the early 1870s.

Blue Water Lilies (Nymphéas bleus)
(1916)

• Oil on canvas, 78.7 in x 78.7 in (200 cm x 200 cm)

Monet, Claude (1840-1926): Nymphéas bleus, 1916. Paris, Musee d'Orsay. peinture Dim. 2 x 2 m. © 2013. White Images/Scala, Florence

Depictions of water lilies were among the most popular, revered, and famous of all Monet's works. During the later years of his life – between the first decade of the 1900s and 1926 – Monet's garden at Giverny, and especially its pond, became his sole source of inspiration. He had originally grown white water lilies to gain pleasure from their beauty, rather than to paint them, but once they began to take shape in terms of becoming established, he was inspired to begin creating them on canvas. He said: "Apart from painting and gardening, I am good for nothing. My greatest masterpiece is my garden."

This particular oil on canvas is a vibrant portrayal of one small area of the pond – a close-up of an exquisite work – yet with little details that stand out. It is a masterpiece in Impressionism that is content to focus purely on the subject matter – there is no sky, no horizon. The painting is contained in its own backdrop; there is no other subject or motif to frame the piece, which gives it a free and timeless approach – Monet, through his sheer brilliance, has given himself the freedom to paint with strong brushstrokes, and the audience a myriad of possibilities in terms of what lies beyond this small section of pond and its water lilies. Commentators state that approaching the work up close gives a feel for the abstract, which inspired many artists in the latter half of the 20th century exploring abstract landscapes.

Bouquet of Sunflowers

(1881)

• Oil on canvas, 39.8 in x 32 in (101 cm x 81.3 cm)

Monet, Claude (1840-1926): Bouquet of Sunflowers, 1881. New York, Metropolitan Museum of Art. Oil on canvas, 39 3/4 x 32 in. (101 x 81.3 cm).
Inscribed: Signed and dated (upper right): Claude Monet 81. H. O. Havemeyer Collection, Bequest of Mrs. H. O. Havemeyer, 1929. Acc.n.: 29.100.107 © 2013.
Image copyright The Metropolitan Museum of Art/Art Resource/Scala, Florence

Bouquet of Sunflowers, completed in 1881, was exhibited at the seventh Impressionist exhibition the following year. The sunflowers for this still life were taken from Monet's garden in Vétheuil, and the painting was revered by critics (who were wowed by his mastery of such a traditional subject) and Vincent Van Gogh, whose own depictions of sunflowers were to be among his own most popular and famous works. However, unlike Van Gogh, Monet painted the sunflowers with no sign of decay. Monet chose seven types of flowers for his still life works – sunflowers were among his most popular – and this work accompanied five others to the Impressionist exhibition of 1882. While Monet traveled throughout Europe to capture the scenes and landscapes that so inspired him, when in financial distress it was the blooms from his own garden that offered him a chance to create his continuing masterpieces.

Camille on her Deathbed

(1879)

- Oil on canvas, 26.8 in x 35.4 in (68 cm x 90 cm)

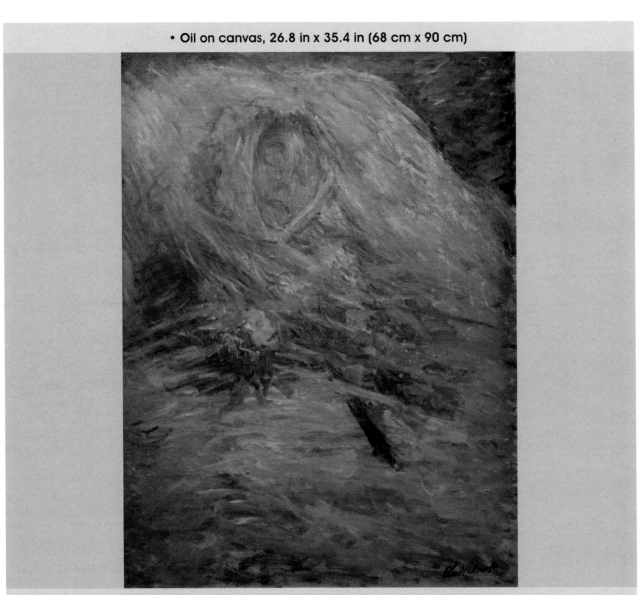

Monet, Claude (1840-1926): Camille sur son lit de mort – Camille on her deathbed. 1879. Paris, Musee d'Orsay. © 2013. Gaspart/Scala, Florence

In 1876, Camille Monet became ill with tuberculosis. When the couple's son, Michel, was born two years later, Camille's health began to suffer yet further. Her body, weakened by illness and pregnancy, quickly began to fade and the tuberculosis took a firm grip, ending the 32-year-old woman's life in September 1879. Monet painted *Camille on her Deathbed* and following her death suffered greatly. He completely dedicated himself to his work after the loss of his wife and some believe that the focus he gave to his paintings helped to create some of the best works of the artist's illustrious career.

This work was in Monet's possession for most of the remainder of his own life, but is highly recognized as one of his most well-known pieces. Camille's death shocked Monet and this piece is a tragic portrayal of losing a loved one. He wrote: "I caught myself, my eyes fixed on her tragic forehead… almost mechanically observing the sequence of changing colors that death was imposing on her immobile face…" At the time of Camille's death, the couple had been living in poverty for a number of years. In addition, Monet had not always treated his wife quite as well as he could. Despite this, Camille was still very dear to the artist who wished to: "record the last image of a woman who was departing forever." Monet described in a letter to a friend how even though he was watching the features of a face he held so dear, he was caught by the color stimuli and the loss of color as life ebbed from Camille.

Etretat, The Cliff, reflections on water
(c. 1885)

- **Oil on canvas, 25.9 in x 32.1 in (65.8 cm x 81.5 cm)**

Monet, Claude (1840-1926): Etretat, la manneporte, reflets sur l'eau, 1885. Paris, Musee d'Orsay. peinture Dim. 0.65 x 0.81 m. ©2013. White Images/Scala, Florence

Monet was inspired by Etretat in the Caux region of Normandy, which he visited every year between 1883 and 1886. He had first come across the area in 1868 and was particularly drawn by how picturesque it was – so much so that it resulted in more than 50 paintings. However, he only painted the Manneporte – the largest of three arches known as the "Gates," twice. When this work was created in c. 1885, Monet regularly met with Guy de Maupassant, a popular 19th-century French writer – often considered one of the "fathers" of the modern short story. Etretat, where Maupassant was living at the time, was the setting chosen for a number of his own works. His thoughts and feelings were mirrored in the works created by Monet of these monumental cliffs and his love of the Normandy coast. Known as the "Elephant and the Needle," due to the rock formations, these famous cliffs are painted by Monet in a typical Impressionist style, with its atmospheric conditions and the effect of the light. The illusion of movement on the sea is carefully created using separate brushstrokes, combined with vibrant colors. Monet was renowned for applying one color over another while the first was still wet – this is evident in this painting through the setting sun.

The work was painted during the winter months, presenting the artist with a number of obstacles, not least the weather, the difficult terrain, and the changing tides.

Haystacks (Effect of Snow and Sun)

(1891)

• Oil on canvas, 25.7 in x 36.3 in (65.4 x 92.1 cm)

Monet, Claude (1840-1926): Haystacks (Effect of Snow and Sun), 1891. New York, Metropolitan Museum of Art. Oil on canvas, 25 3/4 x 36 1/4 in. (65.4 x 92.1 cm).
Inscribed: Signed and dated (lowerleft): Claude Monet 91. H. O. Havemeyer Collection, Bequest of Mrs. H. O. Havemeyer, 1929. Acc.n.: 29.100.109
© 2013. Image copyright The Metropolitan Museum of Art/Art Resource/Scala, Florence

This painting is a depiction of haystacks close to Monet's home at Giverny. For about 18 months, between 1890 and 1891, he focused on the subject matter and created around 30 paintings. As he often found, the changing light during the day presented him with many obstacles in his landscapes, he wrote: "I am… struggling with a series of different effects [haystacks]… but at this season, the sun sets so fast I can not follow it…" He admitted that he felt a great deal of work was necessary in order to succeed with the rendering he wanted. *Haystacks* was the first group of multiple versions of a theme that he exhibited in 1891. Fifteen depictions were shown in Paris at the Galerie Durand-Ruel. The theme was among his most celebrated. Note the delicate visualization of light in this particular piece and the fleeting effects of light and color. The haystacks are captured in winter daylight with violet and orange hues, covered in snow, with a hint of the brown of the hay underneath. It is a vibrant portrayal of a simple yet effective subject showing the artist's brilliance for capturing light.

Hôtel des roches noires, Trouville
(1870)

• **Oil on canvas, 31.9 in x 23 in (81 cm x 58.5 cm)**

Monet, Claude (1840-1926): The Hotel des Roches Noires at Trouville. Paris, Musee d'Orsay. © 2013. Photo Scala, Florence

33

Following their civil wedding ceremony on June 28, 1870, some three years after the birth of their first child, Jean, Monet and Camille stayed in Trouville where he painted *Hôtel des roches noires* depicting a popular and fashionable seaside resort. It was a bold piece for Monet, whom was greatly influenced by Eugène Boudin, although his originality is plain to see. The piece is animated with the illusion of fluttering flags, clouds rolling across the blue sky, and the figures promenading in the left foreground. The main flag draws the audience's attention with its vibrancy and motion. It serves to balance the strong perspectives to the right and bottom of the piece. The strong sunlight creates a shadow from the building. The painting is powerful – creative and lifelike in its portrayal of a tranquil, serene setting, it is inviting and warm, almost willing the audience to take a leisurely stroll along the promenade.

While Monet painted this depiction of the popular hotel, frequented by American tourists, he and Camille spent their honeymoon in Hotel Tivoli, which was rather less expensive and fashionable. In their flight to London, to avoid the Franco-Prussian War, they failed to pay their hotel bill.

Impression, Sunrise

(1872)

• Oil on canvas, 18.9 in x 24.8 in (48 cm x 63 cm)

Impression, sunrise (Impression, Soleil Levant), 1872, Digital by Claude Monet (1840-1926). Paris, Musee Marmottan. © 2013. DeAgostini Picture Library/Scala, Florence

This famous painting, *Impression, Sunrise*, was created from a scene in the port of Le Havre. Monet depicts a mist, which provides a hazy background to the piece set in the French harbor. The orange and yellow hues contrast brilliantly with the dark vessels, where little, if any detail is immediately visible to the audience. It is a striking and candid work that shows the smaller boats in the foreground almost being propelled along by the movement of the water. This has, once again, been achieved by separate brushstrokes that also show various colors "sparkling" on the sea. It is this painting's title from which the Impressionist movement gained its name. A critic analyzing the work described it as an "impression." It was meant as a jibe at the group of young artists breaking with tradition in terms of oil technique, but the name suited the style and it became forever synonymous with the artist and his peers. This particular work was shown at the first Impressionist exhibition in 1874, and is a striking example of the new innovative style.

The painting was signed by Claude Monet, 72, but in actual fact was painted by the artist in 1873, according to the *Catalogue Raisonné*. Although many commentators do not mention it and it is covered in few books about Monet, the painting was stolen from Musée Marmottan, Paris, on October 27, 1985, but was recovered in 1990.

Le bassin d'Argenteuil
(c. 1872)

• Oil on canvas, 23.6 in x 31.7 in (60 cm x 80.5 cm)

Monet, Claude (1840-1926): Le bassin d'Argenteuil, 1872. Paris, Musee d'Orsay. peinture Dim. 0.6 x 0.8 m. © 2013. White Images/Scala,Florence

The river Seine, its boats, visitors, and the surrounding countryside, were a great draw for Monet, especially during the years he lived in Argenteuil. This work, created around 1872, shows his meticulous and incredible attention to light and color. He used fragmented or separate brushstrokes to capture the sunlight filtering through the trees across the path to the left of the painting. The shadows balance expertly across the path on which locals are enjoying an afternoon stroll, while others sit on the riverbank, relaxing and watching the river. The work is luminous and vibrant and includes a road bridge with a toll at each end in the background, a bathing pool, jetty, and washhouse, yet it is the sky that draws the audience's attention as much of the piece is given over to the feather-like clouds rolling across the canvas. The bridge actually had seven arches – here Monet depicts five – and the tolls themselves are higher than they are in reality – Impressionism at its best.

Le Quai du Louvre

(1867)

• Oil on canvas, 34.3 in x 24.4 in (87 cm x 62 cm)

Monet, Claude (1840-1926): Le quai du Louvre a Paris en 1867. The Hague, Gemeentemuseum. peinture. Dim: 0.87 x 0.62 m. © 2013. WhiteImages/Scala, Florence

This exquisite masterpiece was created when Monet asked a Louvre official for permission to work on scenes from the windows of the museum on April 27, 1867. He began work a few days later – after permission was granted – and created three views toward the Panthéon and the river Seine. As was so typical of Monet, the light and shadow are of most interest in this busy portrayal of daily life. The hustle and bustle of the riverbank with its people, horses, and carriages are separated from the magnificent buildings – sitting neatly across the center of the painting by the river and the vibrant trees along its bank. Monet is meticulous in the detail of his subject of urban life, soon to become an integral part of Impressionism. Created from the terrace of the Louvre, Le Quai du Louvre was completed in the same year that Paris became a focus of international attention following the World Fair of 1867. The city had begun to take its modern form after the narrow streets were demolished and replaced by wide boulevards and new quarters, by Napoleon and Baron Haussmann.

In this urban landscape, Monet has turned his back – quite literally – on the old masters in the Louvre behind him and has completed a snapshot of Haussmann's new vision, a new, transformed city. It is likely that the Louvre officials who granted him access inside the building in which to work had thought that like many other artists before him, Monet intended to replicate the works of the great masters. However, he chose instead to create the emerging city with its bright colors while capturing the light that shone across the subject.

This particular piece has the same skyline as The Garden of the Infanta, the first painting of the three, and is similar in size to the other two works. However, unlike the first painting, this (and the second one) was a horizontal landscape.

London, Houses of Parliament.
The Sun Shining through the Fog

(1904)

• Oil on canvas, 31.9 in x 36.2 in (81 cm x 92 cm)

Monet, Claude (1840-1926): The Houses of Parliament in London. Paris, Musee d'Orsay. © 2013. Photo Scala, Florence

In 1900, the Houses of Parliament in London, on the banks of the Thames, were a regular theme in Monet's work. His early works of the theme were created from the terrace at St. Thomas's Hospital, close to Westminster Bridge on the opposite bank. London, famed for its fog, clearly shows the Houses of Parliament filtering through, on a fall or winter day. It is ethereal and ghostly in its approach, while the sky and water of the Thames are painted in purple and orange hues. The piece is composed of color patches that intensify the density of the mist, creating a truly atmospheric painting. Monet was becoming renowned at this time for his use in the freedom of color. The richness of his works was beginning to take shape in a way that would have been unthinkable prior to the early 1870s. This particular piece was completed in 1904, and was one of almost a hundred canvases by Monet around this time. He continued working on these paintings from his studio in Giverny on his return to France.

Luncheon on the Grass

(1865-1866)

• Oil on canvas, 181.1 in x 236.2 in (460 cm x 600 cm)

Monet, Claude (1840-1926): Le Dejeuner sur l'herbe (The Picnic). Moscow, Pushkin Museum. © 2013. Photo Scala, Florence

Luncheon on the Grass was a monumental work begun in the spring of 1865. Manet's painting of the same title had received much sarcasm from the critics and public alike when it was exhibited in 1863 at the Salon des Refusés. Monet – who intended the work as a tribute and a challenge to his friend and peer – abandoned his own version in 1866, just before the Salon exhibition where he had intended to show it.

Two fragments of the work are now housed in the Musée d'Orsay. In 1920, Monet explained how he had needed to pay his rent and he gave the original work to his landlord as surety in the late 1880s. When the artist had enough money to buy back his painting, the time it had spent rolled up in the cellar meant that it was suffering from mold. He cut the piece up in 1884 and kept three fragments. The whereabouts of the third fragment are unknown.

Monet also made a sketch of this work where the most noticeable difference was the replacement of the young man – without beard – sitting on the tablecloth in the sketch to the heavily-bearded man that resembled Gustave Courbet, who was quite taken with the original work. He had seen the work when he visited Monet and Bazille in their shared studio in 1865. However, other commentators argue that it was Courbet's comments that caused Monet to abandon the work. It is possible that Courbet both complimented and criticized the work in equal measure. There are suggestions that Courbet offered Monet a regular critique of the work and that later Monet regretted inviting the artist to give him direction in the work. Even if Courbet – master of the avant-garde – hadn't criticized the sketches, it would have been a huge task for Monet to transpose them into a monumental painting. He was hard pushed to finish it in time for the Salon exhibition and probably put it to one side – a work of this magnitude would have been an expensive undertaking for a young, up-and-coming artist.

Poppies (Coquelicots)

(1873)

• Oil on canvas, 19.7 in x 25.6 in (50 cm x 65 cm)

Monet, Claude (1840-1926): Poppies. Paris, Musee d'Orsay. © 2013. Photo Scala, Florence

This beautiful painting was created on Monet's return from the United Kingdom (in 1871) when he settled in Argenteuil with his family until 1878. It was a time that provided the artist with great fulfillment as a painter, despite the failing health of Camille. Paul Durand-Ruel, Monet's art dealer, helped support him during this time, where he found great comfort from the picturesque landscapes that surrounded him and provided him with plenty of subject matter from which to chose. It was a time that Monet's plein air works would develop, and this particular painting was shown at the first Impressionist exhibition of 1874. This beautifully depicted summer's day is captured in all its glory with the vibrant poppies complementing the wispy clouds in a clear blue sky. The painting has two color tones: the red and the bluish green. The work is clearly a visual impression and the abstract creeps in. Some commentators advocate that the two foreground figures, the woman and young child, are Monet's wife and son. However, the figures are almost incidental to the landscape; it is suggested that they suggest Monet's feelings toward nature and that human life should respect and take care of nature. To some audiences the poppies have a movement to them – perhaps a quiver – while the overall work is certainly an impression of a landscape. Everything here is suggested rather than exact.

Regattas at Argenteuil

(c. 1872)

• Oil on canvas, 18.9 in x 29.5 in (48 cm x 75 cm)

Monet, Claude (1840-1926): Boat Races at Argenteuil, c. 1872. Paris, Musee d'Orsay. Oil on canvas, 48 x 75 cm. © 2013. Photo Scala, Florence

More than 40 years after boating became fashionable, Monet took great care with his depictions of boats of all descriptions. Here, he carefully crafts racing boats on the Seine – they competed at Argenteuil from the 1850s onward – and their magnificence in this masterpiece is a stunning portrayal. Many spectators were brought to Argenteuil for the racing by train – which linked the small rural community to the city. This work is one of around 170 that Monet created during his time in Argenteuil (where more than half include the Seine). He cleverly gives the water movement by fragmenting or separating his brushstrokes. He was seeking to provide the fluidity of the air and water but he did find the ever-changing light a challenge. Despite this, he always beautifully captured the nuances and the vibrancy of the subject and themes he worked on.

Both Monet and his contemporary, Renoir, were fascinated with the sails of the boats that they captured in their paintings. They would often paint the same boats from the same spot and sought to overlook the detail in favor of an abstract rendering of light. Many commentators believe that Monet and Renoir working together helped the two artists to take their creations to new and innovative plains that they may not have achieved if not spurred on by the other.

Rouen Cathedral: The Portal (Sunlight)
(1894)

• Oil on canvas, 39.3 in x 25.9 in (99.7 x 65.7 cm)

Monet, Claude (1840-1926): Rouen Cathedral: The Portal (in Sun), 1894. New York, Metropolitan Museum of Art. Oil on canvas, 39 1/4 x 25 7/8 in. (99.7 x 65.7 cm).
Inscribed: Signed and dated (lower left): Claude Monet 94. Theodore M. Davis Collection, Bequest of Theodore M. Davis, 1915. Acc.n.: 30.95.250
© 2013. Image copyright The Metropolitan Museum of Art/Art Resource/Scala, Florence

This fascinating painting was one of more than 30 depictions of Rouen Cathedral. It is an atmospheric piece, which was probably worked on alongside other canvases of different views of the historic building at the same time. The series of paintings provides an inspiring collection of works of the cathedral at different times of the day and also provides a record of the artist's experiences with light and atmosphere – a fascinating insight into what Monet was actually experiencing. He wrote: "Everything changes, even stone," when referring to the effect the sun had on the façade of the building. A year after this work was completed, it was included in a series of 20 paintings that went on exhibition in the gallery of Paul Durand-Ruel in 1895. Both Cézanne and Pissarro praised Monet's work and eight paintings from the series were bought by patrons.

The Argenteuil Bridge (Le Pont d'Argenteuil)

(1874)

• Oil on canvas, 23.8 in x 31.5 in (60.5 cm x 80 cm)

Monet, Claude (1840-1926): The Bridge at Argenteuil, 1874. Paris, 13 x 18 Musee d'Orsay. Oil on canvas, 60.5 x 80 cm. © 2013. Photo Scala, Florence

In 1874, Monet painted the Argenteuil Bridge on seven occasions – and the railway bridge that spanned the Seine further upriver from the small town. They were part of a large number of his works focusing on the Seine and the reflections of which he was such a master. The color and the light used in this particular work are stunning in their composition, particularly with regard to the sailing boats and the houses in the background on the opposite bank of the river. The orange and blue hues contrast in a beautiful serene way and accentuate the illuminating light. The fragmented brushstrokes, providing a real sense of movement within the water, are carefully applied, giving the river a "choppy" feel. There is a vibrant variety in this painting of solid forms, reflected carefully in the undulating water of the river. There is clear flexibility in the artist's approach to a serene scene. Impressionists were often accused of losing sight of the qualities of form and composition. That is not true in this painting – it is convincing and solid in its approach. As was fairly typical, Monet chose a dappled sky, balancing the rest of the piece simply but beautifully, while the trees are denser. Monet advocated ignoring the objects visible to the painter – concentrating more on the colors that were apparent in the composition of the landscape laid out in front of the artist.

The Artist's Garden at Giverny
(1900)

- **Oil on canvas, 31.9 in x 36.2 in (81 cm x 92 cm)**

Monet, Claude (1840-1926): The Artist's Garden at Giverny, 1900. 13 x 18 Paris, Musee d'Orsay. Oil on canvas, 81 x 92 cm. © 2013. Photo Scala, Florence

By the end of the 1890s, Monet was selling enough paintings to buy his house at Giverny outright. As soon as he did, improvements to the garden began to take shape. It was a passion for Monet who started work on the pond – his water garden – by damming a stream that ran into the river Epte. Although Monet never traveled as far as Japan, he was interested in Japanese styles – the bridge followed in this vain, over the pond, and was given prominence in many of his most famous works of art from around 1900 onward. By this time, the weeping willows and water lilies were all formerly established and provided Monet with the most exquisite of backdrops and colorful themes on which to base his beautiful paintings. The early paintings of the bridge over the pond were the start of an exciting phase both within the garden itself and Monet's carefully crafted works. Between 1903 and 1908, Monet completed 48 paintings of his garden in Giverny. The bridge was later abandoned as his vision and focus moved closer to the water surface, the water lilies, and their reflections. Sometimes there was only a suggestion of the vegetation and other trees in the background of these works, other times they were left completely to the imagination as he concentrated on a small section of the pond and its intricacies.

In this particular work, Monet concentrates on the vivid colors presented in his garden with its purple, mauve, red, green, and brown hues. The depth of the color is striking. As the series of paintings of the garden developed, the artist limited the number of plants within his large canvases, but made them larger and bolder. By the end of the series of paintings, it was the play of light that became their main feature. Here, there are rows of color, in the irises in the foreground with their thick brushstrokes. White highlights the flowers that are blocked from the sunlight by the trees. There is great attention to detail in the garden in Giverny and this work, despite its Impressionist nature, pays homage to this, while the blocks of color would eventually find their way into his water lilies paintings.

(c. 1867)

• Oil on canvas, 25.6 in x 36.4 in (65 cm x 92.5 cm)

Monet, Claude (1840-1926): Road with snow at Honfleur, 1867. Paris, Musee d'Orsay. Painting. 0.65 x 0.92 m. © 2013. WhiteImages/Scala, Florence

Although dated as 1867, this work was given a date of 1865 when it became housed in the Louvre in 1911. It is likely that the later date is, in fact, the correct one, or certainly more likely according to local painter, Alexandre Dubourg. At the time, Monet, along with fellow artists, Courbet, Bazille, Constant Troyon, Charles-François Daubigny, Jean-Baptiste-Camille Corot, Boudin, and Jongkind, spent time at the Saint-Siméon farm where he worked on a number of snow-themed works. It was a quiet spot in Normandy frequented by all these artists in order to further their respective paintings.

This particular work, of Honfleur, followed Courbet's snowscapes – where his typical motif was the stag and the hunter. Monet opted for a more deserted landscape. Here the cart, its driver, and the horse play a minor role. It is the snow and the landscape that it envelops which is the dominant feature. Painting themes covered in snow gave Monet another perspective with regard to light. The changes in color here are extremely subtle, yet they are vivid in their portrayal of the overall scene. It is a tranquil, everyday setting under a winter sky, while the ground, rooftops, and trees are covered in a picturesque and heavy covering of snow. Monet used a limited number of shades, but has still captured the reflections, shadows, and light on his landscape. Monet was taken with the Normandy winter countryside and his snow pieces in the second half of the 1860s pay homage to this. This is an exquisite composition, carefully crafted with colors that "bleed" into one another while creating a beautiful work of Impressionism. Commentators cite that this particular work was greatly influenced by Japanese prints – they gave the effect of bright light reflecting off snow as they were printed with translucent colored inks on light paper.

The Coalmen (also called Men Unloading Coal)
(c. 1875)

• Oil on canvas, 21.3 in x 25.9 in (54 cm x 66 cm)

Monet, Claude (1840-1926): Les dechargeurs de charbons – Unloaders of coal. 1875. Paris, Musee d'Orsay. © 2013. Gaspart/Scala, Florence

This industrial impression of coalmen unloading barges was inspired by Monet's interest in the facets of modern life around him, although it was unusual for him to create a work of this subject matter. Like his contemporaries he was surrounded by fast-moving changes and industrialization. He often traveled to Paris where he would have witnessed scenes on the banks of the Seine, like this one. The painting shows the road bridge at Asnières and the Clichy Bridge (in the background). Unlike his sailing paintings or the scenes he painted from his boat studio, this one concentrates on the workhorse of the river: the barge. As a result, it has a darker approach than many of Monet's works – it is not a criticism of the situation – the fact that the workers are not illuminated (as much because they are under the bridge as anything else), does suggest recognition for their hard work and their plight. It is an illustration of labor-intensive hard work that was carried out every day in the city. Coal was transported from Belgium and Northern France via the Saint-Quentin Canal, completed in 1810. The smoking factories, which the coal was destined for, can be seen in the hazy background. Commentators also cite that there is a clear analogy here with the Japanese prints that Monet collected.

The Doge's Palace seen from San Giorgio Maggiore
(1908)

• **Oil on canvas, 25.7 x 36.5 in (65.4 cm x 92.7 cm)**

Monet was keen, when able, to travel to other cities and regions in order to paint what he saw. He visited Venice, just once, in the fall of 1908. He worked on a relatively small number of paintings while in the beautiful city – there are just 37 canvases. Monet liked Venice but struggled with the subjects and themes presented to him in the city. The "beginnings" that he took home were later completed in his studio. It may have been that so many had already captured the essence of Venice, it might have been because he was already so focused on his works of his garden in Giverny; when he was due to set off for his visit he wasn't even sure that he would paint, but once he arrived he felt an urge to get to work. Monet concentrated on well-known landmarks, including the Doge's Palace – as seen in this work – San Giorgio, da Mula Palace, and the Rio de la Salute. His visit turned into a painting campaign once he discovered the delights of a city based on water. He stayed in the Barbaro Palace on the Grand Canal, a veritable waterway of activity, with his second wife, Alice. The couple rarely left Giverny, so the visit was both pleasant and shocking for them. Alice's letters home to her daughter Germaine Salerou were eventually published by Philippe Piguet (Germaine's grandson) in a book entitled, *Monet et Venise*, in 1986.

Monet's work began in Venice on October 9, 1908, where it was ruled by the daytime sun. Mornings were taken up with the monuments facing St. Mark's Square. He would then turn his attention to San Giorgio, before concentrating on da Mula Palace after lunch. He was enamored with the view from his hotel window – where they moved after their British host had to leave Venice. They were even excited by the electric lighting in the hotel, which meant Monet could continue working into the darkness – they would return home and have electricity installed in Giverny. The couple finally left Venice on December 7, 1908. Alice's health began to deteriorate not long after they arrived home and they never managed to return to Venice. Monet's second wife died three years later. It was virtually two years after leaving Venice that Monet began to complete his 37 paintings.

The Japanese Footbridge
(1920-1922)

• Oil on canvas, 35.2 in x 45.4 in (89.5 cm x 115.3 cm)

Monet, Claude (1840-1926): The Japanese Footbridge, 1920-22. 10 x 12 New York, Museum of Modern Art (MoMA). Oil on canvas, 35 1/4 x 45 7/8 in. (89.5 x 115.3 cm).
Grace Rainey Rogers Fund. 242.1956. © 2013. Digital image, The Museum of Modern Art, New York/Scala, Florence

Monet preferred the earthy tones, and this painting, *The Japanese Footbridge*, is a classic piece of Impressionism in these hues of browns, oranges, maroons, and rusts. The central subject for his paintings in the late 1890s was back within his remit – although its treatment is markedly different. This work was part of the later series made between 1920-1922 and features dense swirls and loose strokes of color. The intensity of the painting almost makes the bridge obscure, while the colors were among those that were unique in his works. Following an accident in 1901 and the temporary loss of sight in one eye, Monet continued to suffer from eye trouble and he developed acute depression (somewhat relieved by his trip to Venice in 1908). However, after the death of Alice in 1911, he was looked after by Blanche, who supported and encouraged him. By the time of this work his eyesight was extremely poor. In addition, his hand was losing its steadiness, giving his works a new approach which, far from being a developing method, was his determination to continue painting at all costs. As a result, this painting is sometimes viewed as lacking the control that his earlier works undoubtedly portrayed. This is an extremely moving piece given the circumstances in which it was created.

The Lunch (decorative panel)

(c. 1874)

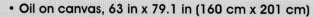

• Oil on canvas, 63 in x 79.1 in (160 cm x 201 cm)

Monet, Claude (1840-1926): Le Dejeuner (The Luncheon). Paris, Musee d'Orsay. © 2013. Photo Scala, Florence

The early large-scale works of Monet gave way to smaller pieces after 1870, but this work, a decorative panel entitled *The Lunch*, was one of the exceptions. It was exhibited in 1876 at the second Impressionist exhibition. It is possible that this work encouraged Ernest Hoschedé to commission Monet to paint panels for his own estate. The portrayal in this magnificent piece is tranquil and relaxed in its approach to everyday life. A small child (Jean Monet) sits and plays by the uncleared table in the picturesque garden. The house is partially hidden by the foliage in the garden.

The Magpie

(1868-1869)

• Oil on canvas, 35 in x 51.2 in (89 cm x 130 cm)

Monet, Claude (1840-1926): The magpie. Etretat, winter 1868-69. 10 x 12 Paris, Musee d'Orsay. Oil on canvas, 89 x 130 cm. © 2013. Photo Scala, Florence

This exquisite snowscape came as a result of Courbet's success with his snow scenes. Monet takes the simple theme of a single magpie sitting on the gate for the focus of his piece. The bird sits as if in contemplative mood in the idyllic landscape setting. The shadows and the light contrast beautifully against the background of trees, ice sky, and snow-covered buildings. There are those that advocate that this is the first "true" Impressionist painting, created five years before the movement was given its name.

The setting for the piece is near Etretat, a landscape of novelty and daring – which was rejected by the Salon of 1869, who said it was "coarse." Notice the exquisite use of white, violet, and gray in order to capture the icy range of colors when presented with a challenge by the sun on snow. Monet would paint 140 winter landscapes – he always advocated he preferred the winter – but this is the largest of his winter paintings. The piece has an almost photographic quality to it despite its Impressionist and innovative approach.

The Rocks at Belle-Ile, The Wild Coast

(1886)

• Oil on canvas, 25.6 in x 32.1 in (65 cm x 81.5 cm)

Monet, Claude (1840-1926): Les roches de Belle Ile, la cote sauvage, 19 eme siecle. Paris, Musee d'Orsay. peinture Dim. 0.65 x 0.81 m.© 2013. White Images/Scala, Florence

Belle-Ile, the largest of the Breton Islands, was little discovered by writers and artists alike. Monet, who sought new landscapes, stayed there for more than two months in the fall of 1886. Here, he wrote: "I am in a wonderfully wild region, with terrifying rocks and a sea of unbelievable colors. I am truly thrilled, even though it is difficult, because I had got used to painting the Channel, and I knew how to go about it, but the Atlantic Ocean is quite different." He found the constantly changing weather conditions and the difficulty in visiting parts of the isle that interested him quite disconcerting. However, he would not be discouraged from his aim and he remained determined to capture the essence of the island.

This particular painting is one of five works and the only one in landscape format. He clearly depicts the battle between the rocks and the sea. This painting, like others, has a photographic quality to it, despite its genre and form. With fragmented brushstrokes and the highlights of white, Monet has captured perfectly the choppiness of the sea around the rocks and the movement of the sea is almost visible to the audience. The blues, greens, and violets in the choppy waters are stunning in their contrast to the rocks. This is a particularly different work to those of Monet's Normandy landscapes. For 10 weeks he stomped his way around the jagged and wild coastline seeking inspiration and variations in light. The canvases from this time marked a turning point in Monet's career. Influenced by the Japanese artist, Hokusai, he began working on a series where he observed and captured a motif at different points of the day – this would remain a crucial influence in his works for the remainder of his life from the 1890s onward. At Belle-Ile he was immersed in nature more than ever before.

The Rue Montorgueil in Paris
(Celebration of 30 June 1878)

(1878)

• Oil on canvas, 31.9 in x 19.7 in (81 cm x 50 cm)

Monet, Claude (1840-1926): La rue Montorgueil a Paris lors de la fete du 30 juin 1878. Paris, Musee d'Orsay. peinture Dim: 0.81 x 0.50 m. © 2013. White Images/Scala, Florence

This striking Impressionist work in 1878, *The Rue Montorgueil in Paris (Celebration of 30 June 1878)*, was twinned with *The Rue Saint-Denis* and was thought to be connected to a July 14 celebration. However, it was painted June 30 for a government festival of "peace and work." It was one of the initiatives organized for the Universal exhibition in Paris and intended as a symbol of France's recovery following defeat in 1870.

This urban landscape is extremely "busy" with its flags expressing patriotism, following such fragility, with colors adding to the vibrancy of modern France and the milling crowd below.

The Saint-Lazare Station (La gare Saint-Lazare)
(1877)

• Oil on canvas, 29.5 in x 40.9 in (75 cm x 104 cm)

Monet, Claude (1840-1926): Saint-Lazare Station. Paris, Musee d'Orsay. © 2013. Photo Scala, Florence

Railways were an incredibly important motif for the Impressionist movement. Here, Monet depicts a piece dominated by smoke, steam, iron, and glass. This particular scene would have been familiar to all the passengers traveling toward the Pont de L'Europe, which can be seen in the background. In the work, a carriage is contained on the left in shadow, while to the right, in the sunlight, are the waiting passengers on the platform. The painting is framed by the roof of the station, which comes to a point in the middle of the top of the canvas, while the smoke from the steam engine below funnels toward its center. Monet returned to the subject in later works and used his works as a commentary on modern society.

At the time of creating this piece he had just settled in Paris – following a number of years painting the countryside around Argenteuil – and began a series of urban landscapes. He desperately wanted to be considered a painter of modern times. However, the permission he gained to work from within the station also gave him instant access to the changing effects of light, movement, and, at the time, a radically modern motif, in the form of clouds of steam. The color in this work is exceptional – and might just as easily be the focus of the piece as the modern motif. Monet painted the station from 1870 at least seven times and these works were a crucial element in his development of Impressionism. Monet's paintings of the station were to be considered the most original in the Rue Le Peletier in 1877.

The Thames below Westminster

(c. 1871)

• Oil on canvas, 18.5 in x 28.5 in (47 cm x 72.5 cm)

In the fall of 1870, Monet traveled to London and this painting is one of a series of works he created while based in the British capital. This view is of the Thames and the Houses of Parliament – covered in other pieces – as seen from Victoria Quay. Like many of Monet's other works, it has a photographic quality to it despite its Impressionist style. Again, Monet uses a fragmented brushstroke to create his magical movement in the river. He also, once again, alludes to the fog and smog that gripped London in the later part of the 19th century. The composition is made up of gray tones, with a pink hue that appears on the horizon. It was while in London that Monet met Paul Durand-Ruel who was to become his most supportive patron. Both Monet and Pissarro – in London to escape the Franco-Prussian War – were intrigued and interested in the city, although their works would prove extremely different in terms of subjects. Pissarro chose the suburbs, while Monet chose the more conventional themes of the Houses of Parliament – as seen here – and Hyde Park.

The Water Lily Pond
(also known as *The Japanese Bridge at Giverny*)
(1899)

• Oil on canvas, 35 in x 36.6 in (89 cm x 93 cm)

Monet, Claude (1840-1926): The Japanese Footbridge and the Water Digitale Lily Pool. Giverny, 1899. Philadelphia, Philadelphia Museum of Art. 35 1/8 x 36 3/4 in. (89.2 x 93.3 cm). The Mr. and Mrs. Carroll S. Tyson, Jr., Collection, 1963. © 2013. Photo The Philadelphia Museum of Art/Art Resource/Scala, Florence

By the 1890s, the financial worries that had plagued Monet for most of his life were coming to an end and he was able to buy Giverny – in fact he had established some wealth and was able to lavish his money on his own home and garden for the first time. It would result in a stunning and unique property, which included the most exciting garden – designed by the artist – and its water lily pond with Japanese bridge. Planning permission was granted in 1893 and he spent much of his focus on the bridge in his works. Incredibly, he only painted about three works of the lily pond up to 1897. This work, from 1899, is exquisite in its composition of background trees, weeping willow, and the bridge, which underwent many alterations up to 1910. The pond here is literally obliterated by vegetation and lilies. It is composed by short brushstrokes – a familiar method during his mature years. In a letter, Monet described how he had planted the water lilies for fun – he had never intended painting them, however, once they established themselves they almost became his only source of inspiration. He wrote: "I saw, all of a sudden, that my pond had become enchanted… Since then, I have had no other model."

The work is part of the series of water lilies – a collection of 13 paintings – although there were eventually 250 paintings of the garden, which he painted obsessively, from the turn of the century until his death in 1926. As already discussed – possibly due to failing sight – the lily pond paintings became smaller in their focus where much of the surrounding backdrop was left to audience imagination.

Train in the Countryside

(c. 1870)

• Oil on canvas, 19.7 in x 25.6 in (50 cm x 65 cm)

Monet, Claude (1840-1926): Train dans la campagne, 1870. Paris, Musee d'Orsay. peinture Dim. 0.5 x 0.65 m. © 2013. White Images/Scala, Florence

This early work – which dates before the formation of the Impressionist movement – is small and encapsulates the natural settings found on the outskirts of Paris. It was typical for painters at this time to choose to paint plein air while restricting themselves to the nature of the city boundaries rather than the rural countryside. The landscape within and on the edges of the larger cities was changing and young painters were keen to capture the new progressions. The railway as an emerging industrial subject was a popular choice for these artists. Monet was no exception and produced this work around 1870. The steam of the engine is clearly visible while the engine itself is not – it is hidden behind a bank of trees. The carriages, however, do feature as a backdrop to a relaxed scene in a cascading park with its dark and bright green hues where locals stroll sedately. It was one of Monet's first railway works and a perfect "snapshot" of life in the early 1870s in his Impressionist style.

Villas at Bordighera (Les Villas à Bordighera)
(1884)

• Oil on canvas, 45.3 in x 51.2 in (115 cm x 130 cm)

Monet, Claude (1840-1926): Les villas a Bordighera en 1884. Paris, Musee d'Orsay. peinture Dim. 1.15 x 1.30 m. © 2013. White Images/Scala, Florence

Monet stayed in Italy on the Mediterranean in 1884, and although inspired by his visit, this work was actually painted in his studio in Giverny, based on another painting, of Villas Bordighera. The work was intended as part of a much larger panel for the drawing room of artist Berthe Morisot's house. It clearly shows the landscape – with its interesting vegetation and foliage – of the region, however, the features are typical Monet. The format is large and square – which he favored for his decorative work – and concentrates on the garden. Monet spent three months in Italy in Bordighera, a popular town on the coast. The coastal town was filled with gardens and palm trees and was a retreat favored by the wealthy British and German travelers. He returned the following year and painted more than 40 more works of the area and its gardens.

Walk on the Cliff at Pourville

(1882)

• Oil on canvas, 25.6 in x 31.9 in (65 cm x 81 cm)

Monet, Claude (1840-1926): La promenade sur la falaise, Pourville, environs de Varengeville; 1882. Chicago (IL), Art Institute of Chicago. peinture Dim. 0.65 x 0.81 m.
© 2013. White Images/Scala, Florence

Monet completed *Walk on the Cliff at Pourville* in 1882 where he visited in Normandy in order to find some escape from personal and professional pressures. It was three years since the death of Camille and he had a new arrangement with Alice Hoschedé whom he would later marry following her husband's death in 1892. At this time, once again, Monet was plagued by financial worries. An economic recession in France had greatly affected the sales of his works and he was less than keen on the forthcoming Impressionist exhibition due to differences within the group. He settled in the fishing village of Pourville for a time and became increasingly encouraged by his new surroundings. Alice and her children joined him during the summer. It is thought that the two young women depicted are Marthe and Blanche, two of Alice's daughters, while other commentators suggest the woman is Alice herself accompanied by one of her children.

Woman with a Parasol, turning to the right

(1886)

• **Oil on canvas, 51.5 in x 34.6 in (131 cm x 88 cm)**

Monet, Claude (1840-1926): Femme a l'ombrelle tournee vers la droite (Woman with Parasol Turned to the Right), 1886. Paris, Musee d'Orsay. Oil on canvas, 131 x 88.
© 2013. Photo Scala, Florence

Monet stopped painting figures after the 1860s to concentrate on landscapes, but he returned to the earlier subject in the 1880s. There are many reasons cited for this decision which seem to center around Monet wishing to use a model to pose for a beach scene with nude bathers. It is reported that Alice was less than thrilled with the idea. As a result, Monet still pursued his desire to paint figures, but chose instead to concentrate on clothed members of his large extended family. An earlier version of this work showed a woman – undoubtedly Camille (accompanied by Jean Monet) – turning to the left. Here the figure reverses the image, minus the child, and turns slightly to the right. It is suggested that the figure here is Suzanne Hoschedé, who was to become his stepdaughter and long-time favorite model.

Women in the Garden (Femmes au jardin)
(c. 1866)

• Oil on canvas, 100.4 in x 80.7 in (255 cm x 205 cm)

Monet, Claude (1840-1926): Femmes au jardin (Women in the Garden), 1867. Paris, Musee d'Orsay. Oil on canvas, 255 x 205 cm. © 2013. Photo Scala, Florence

Monet began a large painting of the garden of the property he rented in the Paris suburbs in 1866. The work was so large that a pulley system was required along with a trench – into which the painting could be lowered on the pulley – so that he could work on the upper areas of the canvas. The aim of this work was to discover how figures – within a landscape – could give the impression that air and light moved around them. He organized this by painting shadows, light with purposely-used color, sunshine filtering through the foliage, and reflections glowing through the darker gloom. Camille, it is known, posed for the three figures on the left of the piece, but the faces of all the figures are left vague and are not composed in a portraiture style. The Salon rejected the work in 1867 for its visible brushstrokes that were considered "deplorable." It was a huge achievement as an early plein air work for Monet, the challenges it had presented were immense, but he overcame them to create this stunning masterpiece.

Monet

In The 21st Century

(PA Photos)

■ **ABOVE:** Sir Timothy Clifford (Director of the National Galleries of Scotland) outside the Monet: The Seine and The Sea 1878-1883 exhibition at the Royal Scottish Academy building in Edinburgh.

Monet's reputation has been so enduring since his death in 1926, that some suggest he became too successful. How so? He is incredibly popular well into the 21st century and there are more Monet exhibitions across the globe today than for many other artists put together. The art critics, for a time, became fairly snobbish about it. However, exhibitions sell-out long before they are due to open and he remains firmly and ludicrously popular. He was an extremely shrewd man who had marketing for his own exhibitions well established. He would carefully arrange his exhibitions with just the right mix of saleable paintings. He would pre-sell paintings to raise expectations and prices. He was a successful investor and lived a comfortable life from the turn of the century at his home in Giverny surrounded by family and servants. Today, it would not be unfair to say that Monet may be judged in terms of numbers as well as for his art. Tens of thousands of people flock to exhibitions every year. A huge amount of money is made from ticket prices and merchandise, and the paintings sell for millions. Monet is still commercial and this is why art critics became snobbish about his work

– the easy on the eye paintings, revered by many who know "nothing" about art according to commentators, caused the critics a slight problem. How could they revere the man who appealed, and still does, to millions? But, surely this is missing the point about how talented, radical, and forward-thinking Monet really was? He was a founder of Impressionism, working in the medium before it even had a name, and he was commentator for his time on the upheavals of France and beyond during the difficult late 19th century and tragic early 20th century. Some commentators argue that his works of London were not merely the creation of historic buildings and monuments but political statements at a time when France was undergoing major political difficulties. At the turn of the century, Monet turned his back on producing patriotic works and spent the later part of his life concentrating on his beautiful water lilies and garden – some say in response to the atrocities of the First World War. He was reacting to the mayhem of the early 20th century. His work was, perhaps, not simply breathtaking, it was emotional. Monet's work is literally exhilarating.

Where to see the works of Monet

The Metropolitan Museum of Art – New York, USA

Mead Art Museum Amherst College – Amherst, USA

Museum of Art – Baltimore, USA

Museum of Fine Arts – Boston, USA

Art Institute – Chicago, USA

Museum of Art – Dallas, TX, USA

Institute of Arts – Detroit, USA

Museum of Art – Kansas, USA

County Museum of Art – Norton Simon Museum – J. Paul Getty Museum, Los Angeles, USA

Museum of Arts – New Orleans, USA

Brooklyn Museum – New York, USA

Museum of Art – Philadelphia, USA

(PA Photos)

■ **ABOVE: One of Monet's *Water Lily Pond* series paintings, c. 1915-1926, at London's Royal Academy, part of the Monet in the 20th Century exhibition.**

Art Museum – Phoenix, USA

Carnegie Museum of Art – Pittsburgh, USA

Museum of Art – Richmond, USA

California Palace of the Legion of Honor – San Francisco, USA

Art Museum – Saint Louis, USA

National Gallery of Art – Washington DC, USA

Kreeger Museum – Washington DC, USA

Musée Marmottan Monet – Paris, France

Musée d'Orsay – Paris, France

The National Gallery – London, UK

National Gallery of Canada – Ottawa, Canada

Musées des Beaux-Arts – Montreal, Canada

Art Gallery of Ontario – Toronto, Canada

(Peter Jordan/PA)

■ **ABOVE: A Christie's employee looks at** *Sur les planches de Trouville* **by Monet. The painting had not been seen by the public for 100 years and sold for $6.9 million at Christie's.**

There are also numerous other museums, galleries, and institutes across the United States, France, the UK, and Germany, as well as other European and international countries which currently house the works of Monet.

Books

Monet or the Triumph of Impressionism by Daniel Wildenstein (October 15, 2010)
Monet by Susie Hodge (March 1, 2010)
Monet by Joseph Baillo and Laurence Bertrand Dorleac (October 1, 2010)
Monet's Impressions by Metropolitan Museum of Art (and Claude Monet) (September 1, 2009)
Monet's Years at Giverny: Beyond Impressionism by Daniel Wildenstein, Charles S. Moffett, and James N. Wood
(January 1, 1998)

(Peter Jordan/PA)

■ **ABOVE:** **Staff at Sotheby's stand by Monet's vision of paradise:** *Water lily pond and path by the water*, **executed in 1900, which went on sale with other Impressionist paintings.**